The Horse Family

CHELSEA CLUBHOUSE

An Imprint of Chelsea House Publishers

A Haights Cross Communications Company

Philadelphia

Bev Harvey

Chelsea Clubhouse
1974 Sproul Road, Suite 400
Broomall, PA 19008-0914

The Chelsea House world wide web address is www.chelseahouse.com

Library of Congress Cataloging-in-Publication Data

Harvey, Bev.
 The horse family / Bev Harvey.
 p. cm. — (Animal families)

 Summary: Simple text compares and contrasts members of the horse family in terms of where they live, body features, eating habits, and size. Species featured include zebras, onagers, African wild asses, donkeys, Przewalski's horses, and domesticated horses.

 ISBN 0-7910-7545-1
 1. Equidae—Juvenile literature. [1. Horse family (Mammals)] I. Title. II. Series.
 QL737.U62H34 2004
 599.665—dc21

                                                    2002155662

First published in 2003 by
MACMILLAN EDUCATION AUSTRALIA PTY LTD
627 Chapel Street, South Yarra, Australia, 3141

Associated companies and representatives throughout the world.

Copyright © Bev Harvey 2003
Copyright in photographs © individual photographers as credited

Edited by Angelique Campbell-Muir
Page layout by Domenic Lauricella
Photo research by Sarah Saunders

Printed in China

Acknowledgements

The author and the publisher are grateful to the following for permission to reproduce copyright material:

Cover photograph: plains zebra, courtesy of Daniel J. Cox—Oxford Scientific Films/Auscape.

ANT Photo Library, pp. 5, 6 (top), 6 (bottom), 11, 17, 19, 20, 25, 26; Australian Picture Library/Corbis, pp. 7 (top), 7 (center), 21, 22; Coo-ee Picture Library, pp. 7 (bottom), 10, 24, 27; Daniel J. Cox—Oxford Scientific Films/Auscape, p. 1; Digital Stock, pp. 14, 16; Kate Drinnan, p. 28; Getty Images, pp. 4 (top & bottom), 8–9, 23, 29; Sarah Saunders, p. 15; Barry Silkstone/Southern Images, pp. 6 (center), 18.

While every care has been taken to trace and acknowledge copyright, the publisher tenders their apologies for any accidental infringement where copyright has proved untraceable. Where the attempt has been unsuccessful, the publisher welcomes information that would redress the situation.

Contents

Animal Families

Scientists group similar kinds of animals together. They call these groups families. The animals that belong to each family share similar features.

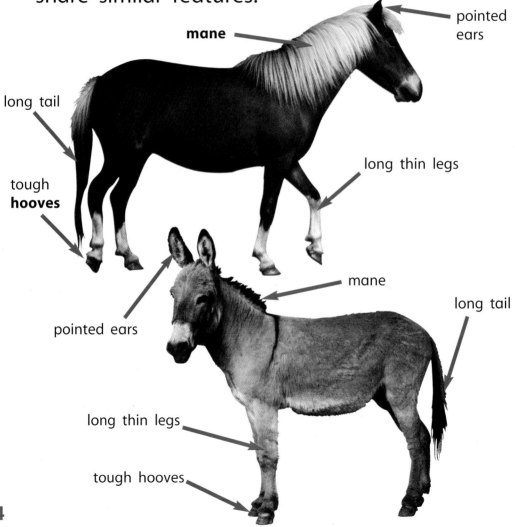

pointed ears

mane

long tail

tough **hooves**

long thin legs

pointed ears

mane

long tail

long thin legs

tough hooves

The horse family

All kinds of horses, including donkeys and zebras, belong to the horse family. Wild horses live in grasslands and deserts. Pet horses live on farms and in **stables**.

Some people keep horses for pets.

Where Horses Live

Grevy's zebras live in deserts and grasslands in parts of southeastern Africa.

Plains zebras roam open grasslands in southeastern Africa.

Mountain zebras are found in mountain grasslands in southwestern Africa.

Onagers live in parts of Asia, including deserts and dry areas of Iran and Mongolia.

African wild asses are found in deserts and grasslands in eastern Africa.

Today, most Przewalski's horses live in zoos. They are **native** to Mongolia.

Horse Features

All members of the horse family have many features in common.

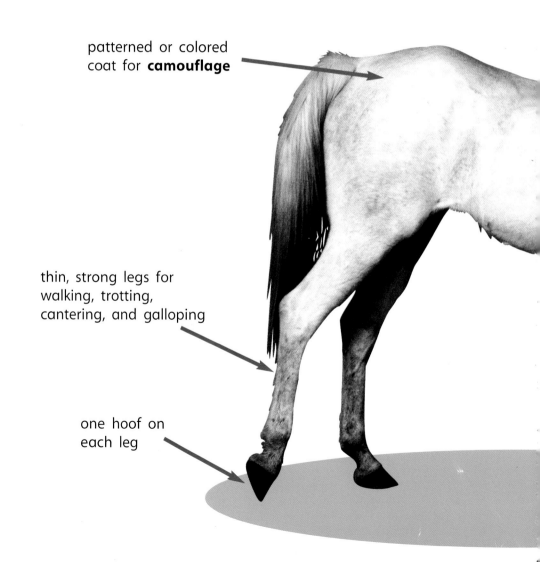

patterned or colored coat for **camouflage**

thin, strong legs for walking, trotting, cantering, and galloping

one hoof on each leg

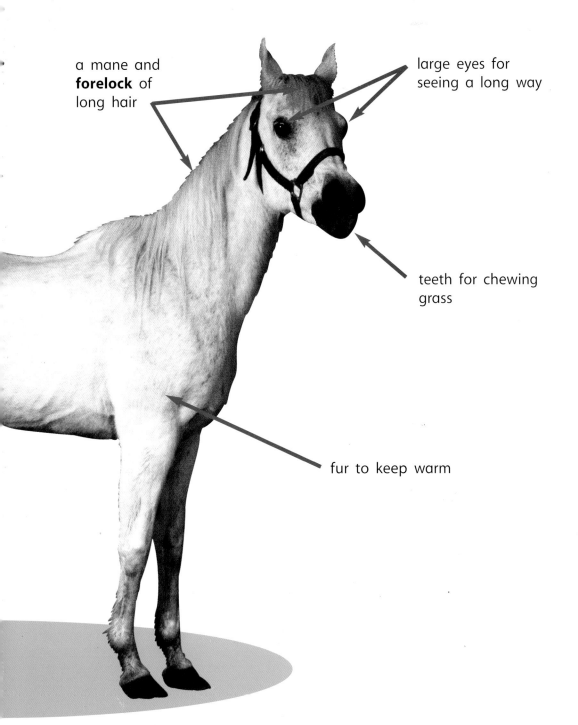

a mane and **forelock** of long hair

large eyes for seeing a long way

teeth for chewing grass

fur to keep warm

Horses as Grazers

Horses stand upright on all four legs. They are fast runners. They have tough hooves so they can run on stony ground as well as on grass.

Horses have strong legs for running.

Pet horses often eat hay.

Horses are **herbivores**. They eat grass, hay, and grain. Wild horses graze on grass throughout the day. **Domestic** horses kept in stables eat hay and grain.

The Size of Horses

Horses vary in size. **Draft** horses are big. Shetland ponies and miniature donkeys are small.

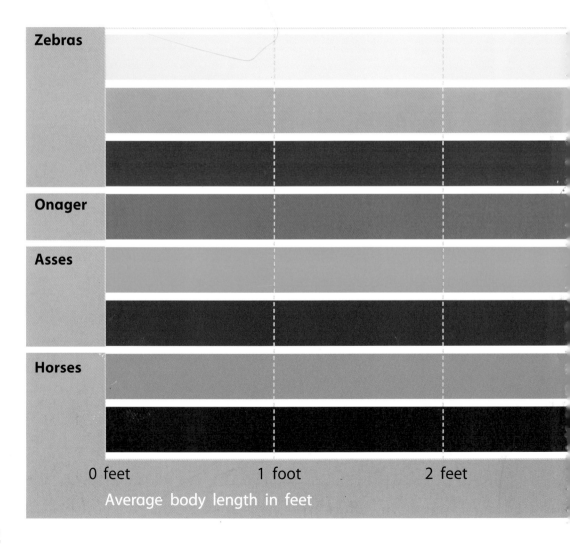

Zebras

Onager

Asses

Horses

0 feet   1 foot   2 feet

Average body length in feet

Horses are measured from the ground to the top of the shoulder.

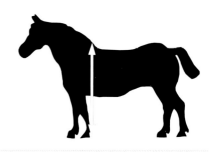

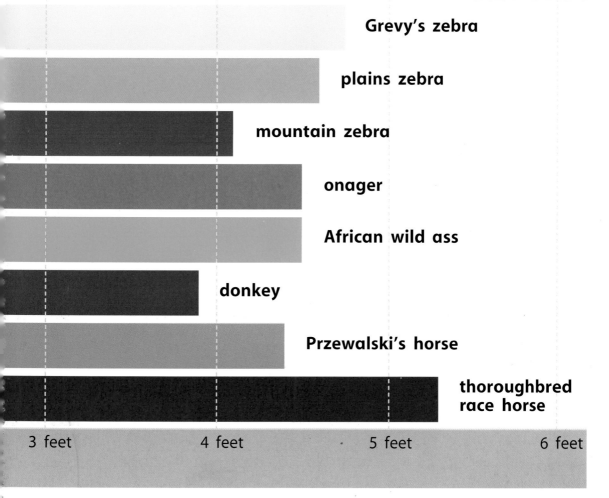

Grevy's zebra

plains zebra

mountain zebra

onager

African wild ass

donkey

Przewalski's horse

thoroughbred race horse

3 feet   4 feet   5 feet   6 feet

Zebras

Zebras live in African grasslands. Their teeth are made for cutting and chewing grass.

Most zebras live in groups called herds.

Each zebra has a unique stripe pattern.

Zebras are covered in black and white stripes. No two zebras have the same pattern of stripes.

Lions hunt zebras.

Lions and hyenas hunt zebras for food. At
dusk and dawn, a zebra's stripes gives it
camouflage. Its stripes fade into the
background and confuse its **predators**.

Grevy's zebras

The Grevy's zebra is the largest zebra. It has thin black and white stripes.

A Grevy's zebra has a larger head than other zebras.

Plains zebras

The plains zebra has lighter shadow stripes between its stripes. A male, several females, and their young make up a family group.

Plains zebras have some lighter stripes that look like shadows.

Mountain zebras

The mountain zebra also has stripes, but it has a plain white stomach. Mountain zebras live in grassy areas in the mountains.

Mountain zebras do not have stripes on their stomachs.

Onagers

The onager was once common in Asia.
People used to kill it for sport and for food.
Now the onager is very **rare**.

Today, only a few hundred onagers are left in the wild.

The onager has a short mane and large ears.

The onager is relaxed and restful when it feels safe. But when it feels threatened, the onager can run faster than 30 miles (50 kilometers) an hour. The onager can jump over high objects and climb steep hills.

African Wild Asses

The African wild ass lives in hilly, stony deserts. Unlike other horses, it does not need to drink water every day. It can survive for up to two or three days without water.

African wild asses have stripes on their legs.

The African wild ass
mostly eats grasses.

The African wild ass is active during the cool
of the morning and evening. When it is hot
the African wild ass finds shade in the hills.

Donkeys

The domestic donkey is related to the African wild ass. Tame donkeys carry people and loads.

Pet donkeys can be trained to pull carts.

A scared donkey may not want to move.

Donkeys are not really stubborn. They just do not like doing anything that frightens them. When donkeys **bray** they make a loud "ee-aw" sound.

Horses

Horses have been tamed by humans for thousands of years. They have been trained to carry people and loads. A horse's body has long legs, a long neck, and a large head.

People ride domestic horses for fun and for work on farms.

Przewalski's horses

The Przewalski's horse is an ancestor of the pet horse. It is short and stocky. There used to be many Przewalski's horses living in the wild in Mongolia. Now they are **endangered** and live on **reserves** or in zoos.

Scientists have started to bring Przewalski's horses back to Mongolia to live on reserves.

Pet horses

There are many pet horse **breeds**. Draft horses, such as Belgians, can pull heavy loads. Shetland ponies are smaller for kids to ride.

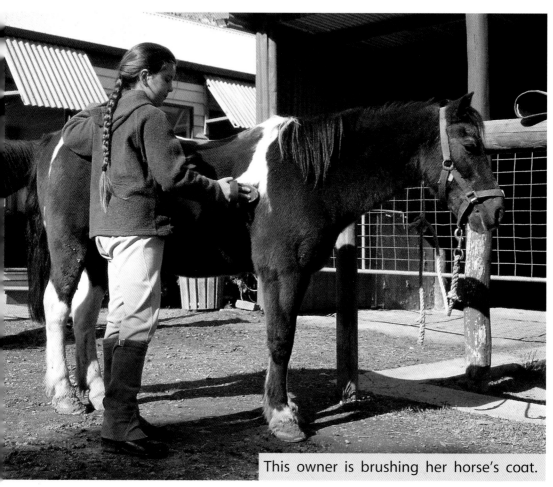

This owner is brushing her horse's coat.

Thoroughbred horses can run very fast.

Some horses are trained for sports, such as horse racing or polo. Some horses are trained to work on cattle ranches. Many people enjoy riding horses.

Common and Scientific Names

The scientific name for the horse family is Equidae. There are nine **species** of horses in the horse family. These are the common and scientific names of the ones in this book:

Equidae family			
Common name	**Scientific names:**		
	Genus	**Species**	**Subspecies**
Grevy's zebra	*Equus*	*grevyi*	
plains zebra	*Equus*	*burchellii*	
mountain zebra	*Equus*	*zebra*	
onager	*Equus*	*onager*	
African wild ass	*Equus*	*africanus*	
donkey	*Equus*	*asinus*	
Przewalski's horse	*Equus*	*caballus*	*przewalskii*
pet horse	*Equus*	*caballus*	

Glossary

bray	the loud cry of a donkey
breeds	types of animals raised by people to look a certain way or to perform certain tasks
camouflage	to blend in with surroundings so it is hard to be seen
domestic	a tame animal that lives with humans
draft	used for pulling loads; draft horses are very tall and heavy
endangered	in danger of becoming extinct, or dying out
forelock	hair that falls over a horse's head between its ears
genus	the name for a large group of similar animals within an animal family; the genus is the first part of the scientific name of an animal
herbivores	animals that eat plants
hooves	the hard covering on the lower part of a horse's feet
mane	long hair growing on the back of the neck
native	to come from a particular country or area
predators	animals that hunt other animals for food
rare	not found very often
reserves	areas of land set aside for animals to live where they are protected
species	a group of animals that are closely related and can produce young; the species is the second part of the scientific name of an animal
stables	buildings to keep horses in

Index